HOW?D THEY DO THAT?

in...

THE PERSIAN EMPIRE

Mitchell Lane

PUBLISHERS

P.O. Box 196
Hockessin, Delaware 19707

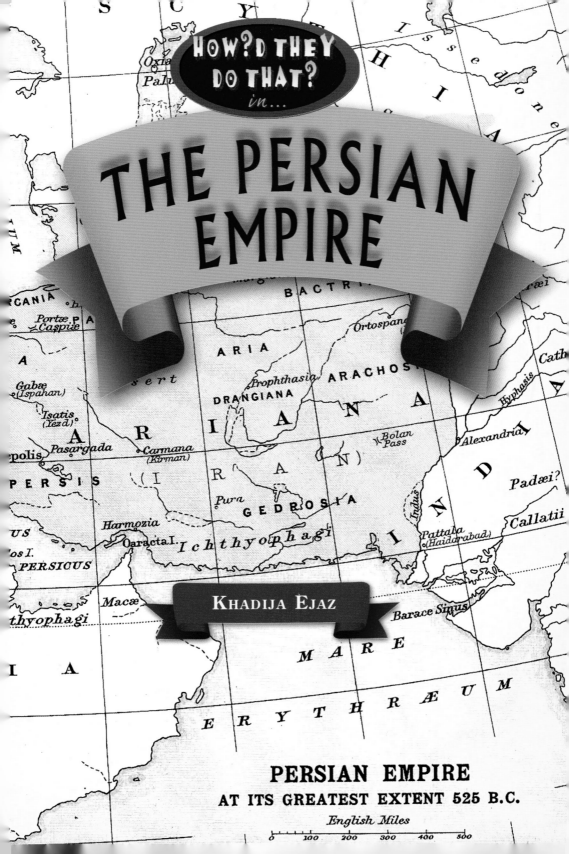

HOW?'D THEY DO THAT?

in...

THE PERSIAN EMPIRE

KHADIJA EJAZ

PERSIAN EMPIRE
AT ITS GREATEST EXTENT 525 B.C.

English Miles

0   100   200   300   400   500

Copyright © 2010 by Mitchell Lane Publishers, Inc. All rights reserved. No part
of this book may be reproduced without written permission from the publisher.
Printed and bound in the United States of America.

Printing   1   2   3   4   5   6   7   8   9

Library of Congress Cataloging-in-Publication Data
Ejaz, Khadija.
  How'd they do that in the Persian empire / by Khadija Ejaz.
      p. cm. — (How'd they do that)
  Includes bibliographical references and index.
  ISBN 978-1-58415-825-7 (library bound)
  1. Iran—History—To 640—Juvenile literature. 2. Iran—Social life and customs—
Juvenile literature. I. Title.
  DS281.E34 2010
  935—dc22

                                                                    2009027345

PUBLISHER'S NOTE: This story is based on the author's extensive research,
which she believes to be accurate. Documentation of such research is contained on
page 61.
    To reflect current usage, we have chosen to use the secular era designations BCE
("before the common era") and CE ("of the common era") instead of the traditional
designations BC ("before Christ") and AD (*anno Domini,* "in the year of the Lord").
    The internet sites referenced herein were active as of the publication date.
Due to the fleeting nature of some web sites, we cannot guarantee they will all be
active when you are reading this book.

                                                                    PLB

CONTENTS

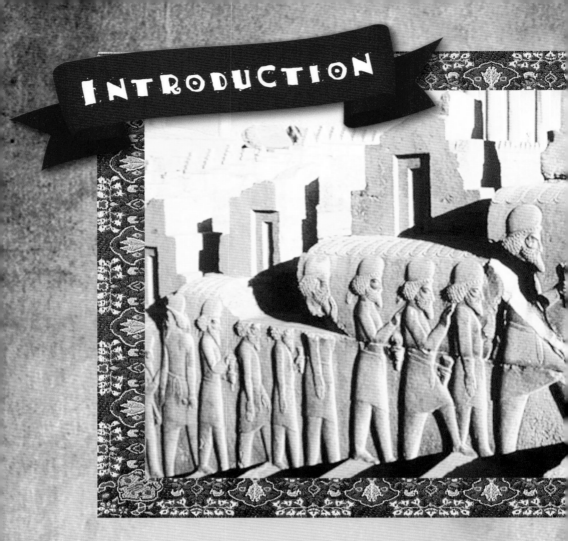

Cyrus held his breath as he beheld the most beautiful woman he had ever seen. So enchanted was the boy, he hardly noticed as the other shoppers at the Persepolis bazaar jostled him. When the woman turned to him, her gold and yellow robes shimmered with the dazzling brilliance of the sun, as if the all-powerful Ahura Mazda himself had woven the silk on his glorious looms. A wavy tendril of long black hair slipped over her shoulder as she extended her right hand to him and smiled. His dark eyes sparkled with the light of the gems she wore on her fingers—deep reds, blues, greens, and purples.

"What is your name, little boy?" she said. Never had the Persian language sounded sweeter.

"Cy-Cyrus," he stammered.

"And what a noble name it is!" she exclaimed. "May Ahura Mazda bless their souls, your parents must have great expectations from you to have named you after such an honorable king!" She pointed to a drinking bowl at the stall of metal wares next to them. "In the spirit of the great renewal of Nowruz, my little Cyrus, I shall buy you this drinking bowl. It has a story of your namesake engraved on it."

The woman handed a gold *daric* to the merchant at the stall and asked for the bowl. He handed it to her, and gave her a few pieces of silver *siglos* in return. These she gave to the boy. If he hadn't known by her appearance before, he knew by her generosity now that this was a woman of great nobility. He lowered his gaze in respect.

Daric

"Thank you, my great lady," he said. "I shall never be able to repay your kindness. My family and I thank you."

The woman nodded. "You're a good son to your father," she said, gathering her skirts. "Now go on. I'm sure you have things to do here before you go home to your family. Loitering will only bring you closer to Ahriman. Light an extra fire in your house this Nowruz to keep his evil forces at bay."

Cyrus bowed to the lady. "I take your leave," he said, and scampered off to find his cousin. He quickly scanned the crowd and caught a glimpse of his father's sister's son at a carpet stall. He dashed toward him, almost running into a few shoppers on the way. But he was hardly sticking out in this bazaar of people who were themselves excitedly bustling about in preparation of the upcoming festivities.

"Parviz!" he shouted, waving his new bowl in the air.

His cousin heard his name and turned from the giant jeweled carpet he was admiring. He looked at the bowl quizzically. "Where did you get that?" he asked.

"A great lady," Cyrus said. He showed Parviz the silver coins. "She also gave me these *siglos!*"

Parviz's eyes shone with excitement. "The ways of the *Bozorgan* are grand," he said. "Surely they are blessed." He put an arm around his cousin. "Let's go buy some sweets from the Shrine of Anahita at the Garden of the Forouhars. I hear the Buddhist traders there have brought some delicious new treats from India this year!"

Cyrus's mouth began to water at the thought of the sweets. The tantalizing aromas from the various food stalls in the bazaar made him long for a syrupy Indian treat. Surely his encounter with the great lady was a reward from Ahura Mazda for having worked extra hard minding sheep with his father last year. He resolved to work harder in the upcoming year.

His daydream was interrupted by the sound of trumpets and horses. The merry crowd parted just as Cyrus imagined the Red Sea had in the story of the Prophet Moses. He re- membered the Jewish traveler who had spent the night at his family's home while on his way to Jerusalem. He had told Cyrus that story. He had also told him how the Zoroastrian king Cyrus had been a friend to the Jews long ago.

The horses trotted through the crowd as Cyrus, Parviz, and the rest looked on in fascination. The soldiers, in their splendid Persian armor, drew shy looks of admiration from the beautiful maidens in the bazaar. Other obviously noble rid- ers were dressed in royal attire. One particularly magnificent- looking rider wore a gold crown embellished with stars and flowers. Parviz whispered to Cyrus that this was the party of the Bactrian satrap arriving at Persepo- lis to pay tribute to the emperor at the royal celebration.

Anahita

At that moment, the little shepherd boy, so humbly named after the legendary founder of the greatest empire in the world, was almost overwhelmed with pride of his heritage. He puffed up his chest and felt his *azadeh* (spiritually free) Persian soul stir within him. "Ahura Mazda, bless us, everyone," he said to no one in particular.

The statue of Cyrus the Great depicts the founder of the Persian Empire in Babylonian costume, a Jewish helmet, wings, and a short Persian beard. The image once bore the sentence, "I am Cyrus the king, an Achaemenian" in three different languages.

HOW DID THEY BUILD THE EMPIRE?

Chapter 1

The Persian Empire was a series of dynasties that ruled over the Iranian Plateau from 550 BCE to 651 CE. At its zenith, the empire encompassed all or most of what later became Iran, Iraq, Syria, Jordan, Israel, Lebanon, Egypt, Turkey, and Cyprus, along with parts of Afghanistan, Pakistan, Turkmenistan, Uzbekistan, Armenia, and Greece.

The Iranian Plateau was home to powerful kingdoms even before the Persian Empire. Entire nations such as Akkad, Elam, Assyria, and Babylon flourished in the region as far back as 6000 BCE. Around 2000 BCE, central Asian nomads called Aryans began to migrate to the plateau. They eventually formed the kingdoms of Medea and Fars (which the Greeks called Persia) in the northwest and south of what is now Iran. The name Iran comes from the word *Aryan,* which means "noble."

The Achaemenid king from Persia, Cyrus II or Cyrus the Great, formed the Persian Empire when he brought Medea under Persian control in 550 BCE. Another great Achaemenid king was Darius I or Darius the Great. The Achaemenid dynasty ruled Persia from 550 to 330 BCE and formed the first Persian Empire.[1]

Persia fell to the Greeks under Alexander the Great in 330 BCE. A Greek general, Seleucus Nicator, took control of Persia after the sudden death of Alexander. The Seleucid Empire was overthrown in 250 BCE by the Aryan tribe of Parni, who founded the second Persian Empire, also called the Parthian Empire. The Sassanid tribe from Fars founded the third and last Persian Empire in 226 CE. They ruled over Persia until the curtains of history were drawn over the Sassanid Empire in 651 CE, when they gave in to the Arab invasion from the south.[2]

GOVERNMENT

The Persians lived under a form of government called charismatic monarchy, which means the kings were believed to be directed by God. This system was established by Cyrus, who believed that kings were blessed with divine favor (farr), and that it was their duty to unite the people of the world under one God.[3] The Persians had great respect for their king as long as he ruled in a just manner.

Darius codified the Persian legal system. He sent his men to Egypt to study Egyptian laws and to set up a universal legal system on their return to Persia.[4] The resulting laws were collectively called the *Data*.[5]

Darius also divided the empire into districts called satrapies. Each satrapy was governed by a satrap, who was often a member of the nobility. A satrapy also had a general to control the army and a secretary of state to oversee administration and collect taxes. All three officials reported to the emperor. They were periodically shuffled and relocated to other satrapies to prevent them from building up power bases.[6]

Successive Persian dynasties more or less retained the system of satrapies. Power in the Parthian Empire, however, was distributed across the provinces. Provincial nobility and feudal lords had an enormous amount of in-

Darius

fluence on the king. In contrast, Sassanid kings tried to return to a more centralized government.[7]

MILITARY SYSTEM

With such a vast empire to govern, Darius instituted a number of revolutionary new methods to keep himself informed. He created a group of inspectors called the Royal Eyes and Ears. These officials journeyed from satrapy to satrapy, listening to the people and reporting their concerns to the emperor. The inspectors also functioned as spies.[8]

A group of 10,000 bodyguards accompanied Darius wherever he went. They pledged their loyalty only to him. They were called The Immortals, because their numbers always stayed the same: If a soldier was ever lost, another was put in his place.[9]

Sassanid Clibanarius

Parthian warfare consisted of guerrilla tactics—they would launch surprise attacks on their enemies or mislead them by pretending to retreat, only to unexpectedly attack them again. Their army included two types of cavalry: heavily armed armored cataphracts and lightly armed, highly mobile mounted archers. The Parthians were especially known for the impressive feat of firing arrows behind them while riding at full gallop in what was called the Parthian shot.[10]

The Sassanid elite formed the two types of heavy cavalry: the clibanarii and the cataphracts. These were further supported by light cavalry, infantry (foot soldiers), and archers. The Sassanid approach to battle involved wearing down the enemy with archers, war elephants, and other troops, then letting the cavalry attack.[11]

PERSIAN ECONOMICS

Darius designed the workings of the empire's economy. He standardized a system of weights and measures. One of his most important achievements was the coin system, which for the first time used two different metals and weights, the gold *daric* and the silver *siglos*, both of which bore his image.[12] This caused trade to swiftly evolve from the basic barter system.

Taxes were the chief source of income for the empire. Most of it was deposited in the royal treasuries and was spent on the maintenance of the army, the administration, and the royal court.[13] The state also derived income from the tributes that were made to the king by the various satraps.[14] The empire also churned a substantial profit from its control over the Silk Route, or Silk Road, which connected the Mediterranean Sea and China.[15]

The Persians dominated the ancient business world. Traders from Byzantium, China, Japan, Armenia, Syria, and Egypt were a common sight in the thriving Persian cities. Raw silk was a major import, and Persian carpets, jewels, rouge, silk, woolen and golden textiles, leather, and pearls were sought after the world over. The Persians boosted trade by building well-patrolled ports, caravansaries (inns for caravans), bridges, and even harbors, linking all the satrapies and the Persian Gulf, India, Central Asia, South Russia, Oman, and Yemen. Chinese paper and silk and Indian spices were taxed upon import, and then were exported to Europe. The Sassanids even used special labels on their goods to promote their brands and distinguish between different qualities, much in the style of famous brands today.[16]

The Achaemenids were the first people to have a system of insurance. Any gifts that were presented to the king were registered in notary offices, and a fair value was assigned to them. Thus, whenever the person who had presented the gift needed any help, the king would oblige.[17]

FYInfo

Some scholars believe that Cyrus cemented his reputation as a champion of human rights when he issued his decree in cuneiform on a clay cylinder in October 539 BCE, when he marched into Babylon.[18] While some may hail the decree, now called the Cyrus Cylinder, as the first declaration of human rights and others may

debate its historical and political interpretation, almost all agree that Cyrus was a benevolent and just ruler.[19] His ability to understand and appreciate other cultures set the tone of the Persian Empire for a thousand years to come when he issued these words:

> I did not allow any to terrorize the land of Sumer and Akkad. I kept in view the needs of Babylon and all its sanctuaries to promote their well being. The citizens of Babylon . . . I lifted their unbecoming yoke. Their dilapidated dwellings I restored. I put an end to their misfortunes.[20]

No prisoners were taken. Cyrus was greeted by the people, who spread a pathway of green twigs before him as a sign of honor and peace. Cyrus set the Jews free from three generations of imprisonment and let them return to their temples in Jerusalem.[21]

The world's first great emperor chose to exercise his divine rights by treating victims benevolently, honoring their gods, and setting higher standards for kingship. His actions were fueled by his religious belief that it was his duty to reign with justice and peace, something he felt he owed to God. From then on, the people of the Iranian Plateau expected their king to be the perfect man.[22]

Cyrus died in 530 BCE. His tomb at Pasargadae bears the words: "O man, whoever you are and wherever you come from, for I know you will come, I am Cyrus who won the Persians their empire. Do not therefore grudge me this little earth that covers my body."[23]

Pictures of the ancient Persian prophet Zoroaster often show him wearing white robes similar to the ones worn by Zoroastrian priests today. Zoroaster, whose family name was Spitama, is usually shown gazing up toward the heavens and is rarely ever shown looking directly at the viewer.

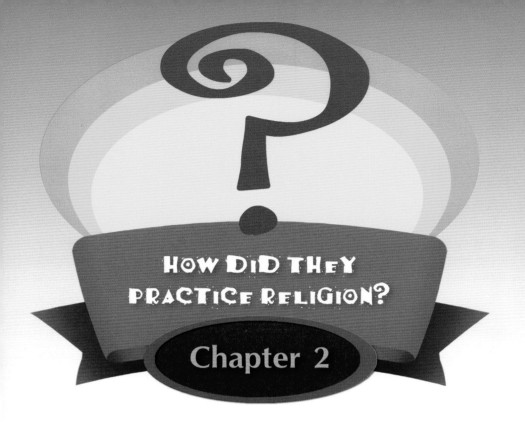

HOW DID THEY PRACTICE RELIGION?

Chapter 2

Sometime between 1000 and 600 BCE, a new prophet was born in eastern Persia. His name was Zarathushtra, but the Greeks called him Zoroaster.[1] He was born at a time when tribal religions were numerous and people worshiped the forces of nature. Rituals were mostly sacrificial and centered on the use of a drug called *haoma*.[2] Personal visions of God compelled Zoroaster to spread his message across the land. Exiled for his views, he sought refuge in the court of a Bactrian king, who helped him spread his word. He met with strong opposition from certain groups of people, and some say that he was murdered while in prayer in a temple.[3]

The religion that Zoroaster preached survives today. Zoroastrianism is one of the oldest monotheistic religions in the world, and it influenced a lot of the religions that came after it. Zoroastrianism introduced the concept of Dualism by preaching the existence of an all-powerful force of good called Ahura Mazda alongside the evil force Ahriman (or Angra Manyu, from which the word *anger* comes). Ahura Mazda is often represented in Achaemenid art by a winged disk with a human figure holding a ring or flower. He is described in inscriptions as "the great god" or "the greatest of gods."[4] Zoroaster believed that humans have the free will to choose between right and wrong, and he stressed the need for people to act righteously and to speak the truth.[5]

Zoroastrians also believe in the existence of divine entities that surround Ahura Mazda. These entities are collectively called the Amesha Spenta, and they were created to protect the world from Ahriman. Guardian angels called Forouhars were also created to protect humans.[6] Zoroaster further preached that a number of saviors would come to the world until the very last one, Saoshyant, who would save the world and bring the resurrection (rebirth).[7]

The fire temple at Yazd, Iran, maintains the Atash Behram ("fire of victory"), the highest grade of fire according to the Zoroastrians. There are nine Atash Behram temples in the world today: eight in India and one in Iran. Fire temples were first constructed in the Sassanid Empire for the reverence of fire, which has always represented Ahura Mazda to the Zoroastrians.

While Zoroaster frowned upon certain religious practices of his time, such as sacrifices and the use of *haoma,* a lot of those practices were reintroduced into Zoroastrianism in the Achaemenid Empire by the Magi, who were the priestly class from Medea. They also reintroduced several of the older pre-Zoroastrian gods, such as Anahita (the goddess of water) and Mithra (the god of the sun).[8]

Persian kingship was a divine responsibility granted by Ahura Mazda. A relief at Taq-e-Bostan illustrates this belief. The Sassanid King Ardashir II (center) is shown receiving a diadem, or royal crown, from Ahura Mazda (right) under the protection of Mithra (left), who is holding a barsom, the saber of justice. The slain Roman under the feet of the king represents the defeat of evil, or Ahriman.

Cyrus and Darius were devout Zoroastrians. They believed it was their duty to rule benevolently under obligation to Ahura Mazda. Zoroastrianism was the accepted religion of the Achaemenids, but it became official under the Sassanids.[9] The Magi rose to immense power during that time. The sacred book of the Zoroastrians, the Avesta, was also compiled then. It contains the Gathas, hymns composed by Zoroaster himself.[10]

OTHER PERSIAN RELIGIONS

A branch of Zoroastrianism that started in the Parthian Empire is Zurvanism. Its belief structure was similar to that of Zoroastrianism, except the all-powerful god was Zervan, and he battled directly with Ahriman. This religion was popular in Medea.[11]

The Sassanid prophet Mani brought Manichaeism to the Persian Empire. A Babylonian by birth, Mani claimed he had visions that made him leave home at the age of twenty-four to preach his message. Like Zoroaster, he received favor from a king, Shapur I; and also like Zoroaster, when the next king took the throne, he and his followers were persecuted. Mani was executed and then crucified.[12]

Mazdak

At the end of the fifth century, a new prophet, Mazdak, preached that men and women were equal. He believed that all the evils of the world came from hating those in different societies, or from different social classes. Mazdakism fought for the rights of the poor and downtrodden. The religion became more revolutionary as time went by and posed a threat to the upper crust of society. The Mazdakites were persecuted until they went into hiding and died out.[13]

FYInfo

Zoroastrians Today

What happened to the Zoroastrians after the Arabs brought an end to the Persian Empire in 651 CE?

Freshly motivated by the spirit of their new religion, the Arabs brought Islam to Persia. In the years that followed, a slow but steady social pressure to convert to Islam caused the number of Zoroastrians in Persia to dwindle. More and more people moved to other regions, most notably to the Indian subcontinent. The natives of India called the new Persian immigrants Parsis. Today, the largest population of Parsis is found in India, with smaller populations in Pakistan and Iran. The Zoroastrian diaspora also extends to Western countries, including Great Britain, Canada, and Australia. These people are descendants of the ancient Persians, and there are only about 17,000 in Iran and 90,000 in India.[14]

Despite their small numbers, the Zoroastrian community is quite active in the modern world. Zoroastrians have one of the highest literacy rates of any community in India at least, and they form one of the most affluent ethnic groups in that country. One of the most famous Zoroastrians of our time was Freddie Mercury, lead singer of the British rock band Queen. You may have come across his performances in the songs "We Are the Champions" and "We Will Rock You." Freddie's real name was Farrokh Bulsara, and he was born in Zanzibar (now part of Tanzania). Other successful members of the modern Zoroastrian community are Indian industrialist Jehangir Ratanji Dadabhoy Tata; music conductor Zubin Mehta; British actor and film producer Ray Panthaki; nuclear scientist Homi J. Bhabha; and photographer and screenwriter Sooni Taraporevala.

Statue of Freddie Mercury

Qanats

Besides guaranteeing a constant supply of water even during dry years, qanats were also used for storing drinking water, providing cooling using wind towers, and storing ice. These sturdy water channels have outlasted natural disasters and wars and can still be seen in ancient cities like Persepolis.

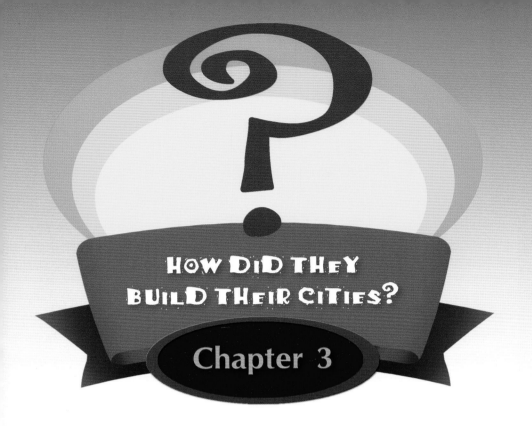

HOW DID THEY BUILD THEIR CITIES?

Chapter 3

Ancient civilizations were often established near a source of water—Egypt on the Nile, the Indus Valley on the Indus River, Mesopotamia between the Euphrates and Tigris rivers. At first glance, the climate and geography of the Iranian Plateau may have seemed utterly inhospitable to any form of human settlement. Rainfall in that region averages only about 12 inches a year. How did the ancient Persians work around that?

The answer can be found in the *qanat* system. The early Medeans and Persians recognized the importance of the availability of water to their cities. They devised a system of underground channels that captured water directly from water tables at the foot of the snow-capped mountains and carried it to the plains. This water supply was vital for the largest industry in Persia: agriculture. An aerial view of *qanats* reveals a series of small depressions across the desert, regularly punctuated by access wells. These shafts emptied into the underground channels. Some *qanats* are many miles long and were dug nearly 1,000 feet (300 meters) below the surface.[1]

Although some *qanats* have collapsed since antiquity, others have remained essentially unchanged since the time of the ancient Persians, and new ones have been built. Present-day Iran has an estimated 50,000 working *qanats*. The use of *qanats* grew popular in the Middle East as well, and they are still used in such countries as Oman.

The ancient Persians also used deep concrete gutters called *joobs*. These narrow canals bordered city streets, channeling melting snow from major mountain ranges.

The Sassanids introduced dams in the third century CE. The first bridges with sluice gates were built to irrigate the plains of Khuzestan. The elaborate Khaju Bridge at Esfahan also has gates. It not only serves irrigation purposes, but also controls the volume of water in the river.[2]

MAJESTIC ARCHITECTURE

Persian architecture is very simple, but it is decorated with intricate designs and bold colors. Buildings constructed in that era typically have

The Khaju Bridge was constructed upon the foundations of an older bridge around 1650 CE during the reign of Abbas II. The upper level can be accessed by both pedestrians and cars, while the lower level provides a shady place for people to relax.

a courtyard and covered arcades, rectangular entrance porticoes, and *iwans*, which are vaulted hallways that lead to the courtyard. Another typical Persian feature is the dome, which Persian architects pioneered during the Sassanid period.

The royal cities of Persia are a legacy of this ancient architectural style. Persepolis, for example, was started by Darius in 520 BCE and continued by successive rulers for another 100 years. It contained palaces, audience halls, gateways, and other buildings. The expertise of artisans from all over the empire was used in building this magnificent capital. Pasargadae was a capital city of Cyrus's and is the site of his tomb. The city boasted two palaces, a sacred precinct (town center), a citadel, and a tower.[3]

The Parthians' architectural style mirrored the Assyrian and Babylonian tradition of barrel vaults, heavy walls, and small rooms. Sassanid architecture was radically different in that walls were built of burnt brick or small stones bound with mortar. Barrel vaults of brick were used to span rooms and corridors, and domes were erected over large halls.[4]

Common people lived in houses made of mud brick, stone, and timber. Bitumen, a black sticky substance also known as tar, was used as a common adhesive, a waterproofing sealant, and a mortar for binding bricks. Roofs were made of timber beams covered with reed matting, a layer of lime, and then a thick layer of mud. Mud or lime plaster was used to make the walls smooth; they were then decorated with paint or colored washes. The earthen ground floor would be covered with reed matting or simply swept smooth. Upper floors were covered with wool carpets, furs, or felt blankets. Two-story houses were popular, with external or internal staircases connecting the different floors. It was not uncommon for an entire extended family to live in one house.[5]

Ancient Bam

THE PERSIAN GARDEN

No Persian city was complete without rich gardens. The Persians, in fact, may very well have founded the discipline of landscape gardening: what is thought to be the oldest garden in the world belonged to Cyrus. In the craggy terrain of the Iranian Plateau, these lush oases were like portals to Heaven, and it is no coincidence that the Persians attempted to re-create what they thought Heaven looked like in the way they laid out their gardens. The word *paradise* comes from *Pardeiza*, which is Old Persian for "an enclosed area."[6]

Persian gardens were laid out in a geometrical pattern inside a walled area. They contained fragrant flowers, lush fruit trees, and babbling brooks. Plane and cypress trees gave cool shade from the Persian sun, while roses and jasmines perfumed the air. Trees and vines laden with figs, dates, grapes, peaches, pears, and pomegranates completed the picture.[7]

These gardens became an important part of Persian culture and were much copied the world over. Not only did they become a fixture in the cities of Pasargadae, Persepolis, and Susa, but they provided important political, philosophical, and religious symbolism. A king who brought a vision of Paradise to his subjects on Earth made a powerful statement about his authority, fertility, and legitimacy.[8]

As a result of the Persians' interest in gardening, the administration greatly encouraged interest in horticulture (growing garden plants), agronomy (crop farming), arboriculture (growing trees and shrubs), and irrigation. Many types of plants were introduced to the empire through these endeavors.[9]

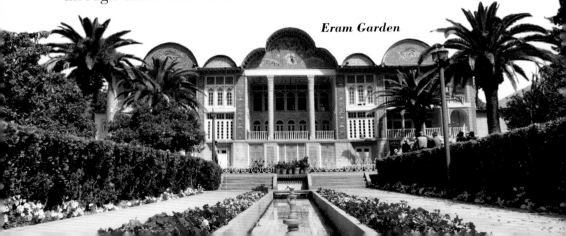

Eram Garden

Ancient Highways

Roads and highways are like the backbone of a nation. Without a way for people to travel quickly and efficiently, entire industries can come to a standstill.

Maybe this is a thought that occurred to Darius when he commissioned the construction of a 1,550-mile (2,500-kilometer) highway during his reign in the Achaemenid Empire. The most impressive stretch of road was called the Royal Road, which connected the cities of Susa and Sardis.[10]

One cannot overestimate the significance of a well-oiled transportation system to a nation. The highway provided a means for the different satrapies to connect to one another. This especially helped state officials travel between regions to keep the king updated on events in his empire.

Stations were set up at regular intervals on the highways where travelers could rest and draw rations. Relays of mounted couriers could reach the remotest areas of the empire in fifteen days, all thanks to the well-organized highway system.[11] This especially benefited the Persian postal system, the oldest in the world. The words of an ancient Greek philosopher, Herodotus—"Neither snow, nor rain, nor heat, nor darkness of night prevents these couriers from completing their designated stages with utmost speed"—praise the Persian postal system. His words inspired the unofficial motto of the United States Postal Service.[12]

Trade and commerce in the Persian Empire received a boost because of the highway system. The Sassanids made a huge effort guarding the caravans that traveled along the highways and even benefited from toll taxes. Many roadways of the famed Silk Route coincided with the Persian highways, connecting Persia to the far reaches of the ancient world, from Japan to Greece.[13]

Persian wine is prominently featured in local mythology and poetry. The wine-drinking tradition is frequently depicted in small paintings called Persian miniatures, a form of art that was adopted from the Chinese.

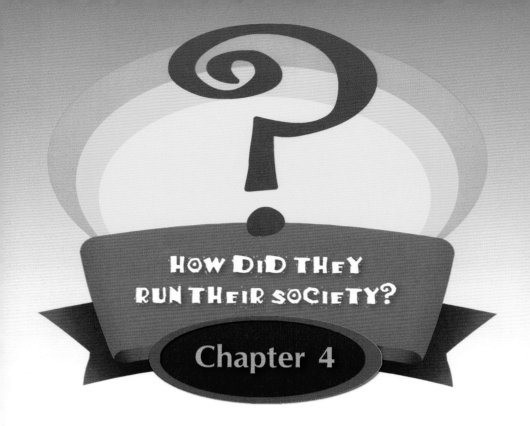

HOW DID THEY RUN THEIR SOCIETY?

Chapter 4

Persian society was inspired by the Zoroastrian concept of good thoughts, good words, and good deeds. The key to etiquette, or *adab,* and to a healthy life was moderation. For instance, the Persians liked to stop eating when their appetites were almost satisfied. Wine-drinking was used to bring happiness and relaxation, but drunken behavior was unacceptable.[1]

Etiquette was also practiced with family, friends, guests, and even strangers. The young respected their elders. Sons would greet their fathers by kissing their hands and feet, and the fathers would return the affection by embracing their sons' heads. Hosts would inquire about their guests' journeys and would go to great lengths to make sure they were comfortable. A host would greet his guests at the entrance of his home. When the guests departed, he would accompany them for several stations along the next part of their journey.[2]

The Persians made conversation into an art. Listening was encouraged over speaking, and everyone tried to speak eloquently. Interrupting another was considered impolite, and apologizing was not looked upon as a sign of weakness. It is important to note that while good manners and being accommodating were considered marks of cultivation, being too agreeable or constantly humbling oneself was not encouraged.[3]

You may have heard of the Seven Deadly Sins. The Persians had their own version in the ten demons. These were the enemies of good life: greed, excessive needs, envy, disgrace, revenge, anger, slander, insincerity, lack of knowledge of religion, and ingratitude.[4]

A COMPLEX SOCIETY

By the time the Sassanids rose to power, Persia had evolved into a highly complex society. The *Shahanshah* (king of kings) reigned above

Persian girls had strong role models to look up to. Warrior women like Pari Satis ("angel-like"), Sura ("flower-faced"), Banu ("lady"), and Azad ("free") bravely defended Persia from its enemies, while political trailblazers like Azarmidokht ("youthful girl") and Purandokht ("beautiful girl") ruled Persia as empresses. Artadokht ("truthful girl") served as secretary of the treasury in the Parthian Empire.

the lesser kings, absolute in his power and a shining light to his people. He ruled with his queen, the *Banebshenan banebshen* (queen of queens).[5]

The rest of Persian society was divided into rigid classes: priests (*atorbanan*), soldiers (*arteshtaran*), scribes (*dabiran*), and commoners (*vasteryoshan-hootkheshan*). Class membership was determined by birth, and barring the rare exception, changing one's class was not possible.[6]

Royal princes, petty rulers, great landlords, and priests formed the *Bozorgan*, the noble class. This mix of established clans and aristocratic families from across the provinces formed the privileged sect of Persian society. The Magi especially had a lot of influence at the royal court by the time of the Sassanid Empire.[7]

Lower classes were divided into freemen (*Azatan*), descendants of ancient Aryan conquerors, and the mass of originally non-Aryan peasantry. The *Azatan* worked as low-level administrators, and they rode in the cavalry in the Sassanid army.[8]

Women were given immense respect in Persia. Zoroastrianism considered women equal to men, and as a consequence, women often held important positions in Persia. Women could be priestesses, monarchs, warriors, and anything else they desired. They enjoyed great social, legal, and economic freedom. They even had the right to choose their spouse.[9]

THE ART OF DINING

Banquets were a grand affair in Persia. An enormous amount of effort went into determining menus and seating plans, and in preparing succulent dishes. Food was served by a battalion of servants. The rituals accompanying these feasts were equally elaborate.[10]

A banquet was composed of several different courses. Fruit, nuts, and saffron were the most popular ingredients. A typical royal menu included sweet grape jelly, candied turnips and radishes prepared with salt, and candied capers with salt from which delicious stuffings were made. The wealth of Persia allowed meat to be a regular part of meals, while it was a luxury in Babylon. Birthdays were celebrated especially

The Persians used gold and silver tableware, such as fluted bowls and rhyta—drinking cups shaped like animal heads. Other items such as jewelry, weapons, and cosmetic containers were also fashioned out of metal and decorated with floral, geometric, and animal designs.

lavishly. Dessert was an important part of the meal, a concept that didn't exist even in Greece.

Meals were served in ornate bowls. The Persians were fond of gold and silver vessels that were fashioned by skilled craftsmen from places like Egypt and India. Tableware also included rhyta (drinking vessels), jugs, strainers, ladles, and scoops.

Persians invented the art of winemaking. The southwestern Persian town of Shiraz is still popular for its grapes and wine.[11] Wine drinking became an important part of public banquets, where guests sipped through straws, deep bowls, or rhyta.

The Persians grew a lot of their own food. Common crops were cereals (barley, rye, millet), legumes (lentils, chickpeas), forage (alfalfa), fruit (grapes, figs, dates, nuts), and vegetables.[12] Poultry and fish were regularly consumed. Beer was brewed from dates and barley.[13]

Ethics in Persia

Imagine a society that regards telling the truth as a virtue greater than beauty, wealth, or power. In our modern world, lying is frowned upon. In ancient Persia, however, it was considered the ultimate disgrace, an act so vulgar that it was equivalent to committing a heinous and violent crime in our time. This centuries-old love affair with the truth has been the proud foundation of Persian society.

The Persians had a reputation for high moral standards in the ancient world. Records recovered from the ancient Greeks, Chinese, Indians, and Arabs offer proof that the Persian people's devotion to the truth was unique. So high was the esteem in which the truth was held that Persian parents often reflected it in the way they named their children. Some examples of names are "protector of truth" (*Artapana*), "lover of truth" (*Artakama*), "truth-minded" (*Artamanah*), "possessing the splendor of truth" (*Artafarnah*), "delighting in truth" (*Artazusta*), "pillar of truth" (*Artastuna*), "prospering the truth" (*Artafrida*), and "having the nobility of truth" (*Artahunara*).[14]

The monarchy derived great inspiration from the truth. Darius's admiration for the truth can be seen at the Behistun inscriptions: "By the grace of Ahura Mazda I delight in what is right; I do not delight in what is false. It is not my desire that the weak should be mistreated by the mighty, nor that the mighty be treated wrongly by the weak. What is right and truthful is my desire."[15]

Behistun Inscription

Persian fashion wasn't simply a matter of appearing stylish. Dress codes were based upon religious rules which guided people on the proper way to wear their hats, robes, and shoes. The Persians liked to dress neatly and wear perfume. Even back then, cleanliness was considered next to godliness.

Before there was Milan, New York, or Paris, there was Persia. The Persian people put a lot of thought into their appearance, and their fashions were quickly adopted in lands as far as Egypt. Even some of the Christian saints of the Middle Ages followed Persian haute couture.[1]

The Persians, even the peasants, were very class conscious and aspired to dress above their social stature. They wore dazzling colors: reds, yellows, blues, greens, oranges, purples, gold, and silver. Colorful patterns were printed on woolen, silk, and linen cloth using carved blocks. The Persians learned the art of silk-weaving from the Chinese and put their own unique signature on it. Sassanid silk was in great demand in places like Byzantium, China, and Japan.[2]

It was not unusual to see Persians making gifts of expensive clothing. The monarchy even was in the habit of donating its fine garments with a change in season. The lucky recipients would be the royal attendants, special people of the court, and other people according to their position in society. Persian royalty did not see a need for summer dresses in winter and vice versa and considered it beneath their dignity to have to hide off-season clothing in their treasury.[3]

Social etiquette extended to clothing and personal hygiene. It was recommended that a person not go out in public with wet hair, wearing only one layer of robes, or without proper footwear. It was polite to remove one's hat in the presence of nobility or in situations of repentance or mourning.[4]

Persian earring

PERSIAN ACCESSORIES

Fashion gurus believe that accessories can make or break an outfit. The Persians believed in that adage wholeheartedly and spent a lot of time matching their rich garments to the right accessories. The exquisite jewelry of that time is a testament to the skill of their craftsmen and to the wealth of Persia. The interest in accessories was not limited to the women, either; both sexes took equal delight in wearing expensive ornaments.

Gold griffin bracelet

Jewelry was often inlaid with a dazzling array of multicolored pieces of stone, glass, faience, and enamel. Popular stones were turquoise, cornelian, onyx, rock crystal, agate, lazulite, and mother-of-pearl. Earrings were generally flat disks with designs made of intricate gold wire. Bracelets and metal collars or chains called torcs, with animal heads on the ends, were popular too. Rings were made of bronze, silver, and gold. The Persians used thousands of other ornaments,

some of which were necklaces, pendants, tiny pins, beautiful glass beads to defy ill omens, ornamented belts and fasteners, fetters (to bind the forehead), and hair holders.[5]

Popular images on jewelry were those of animals, including lions, rams, goats, and ducks. An inlay was sometimes used to create the effect of a mane of a lion. Mythological and herbal images were popular too. Achaemenid bracelets, for instance, were adorned with the heads of lions, rams, geese, deer, and snakes.

Ornaments were even sewn onto clothing. Gold roundels (circular jewels) and plaques were often attached to textiles to add a new level of detail to Persian fashion.

PIONEERS OF BEAUTY

The Persians loved flowers. Not only were flowers an obvious staple in the famed Persian gardens, but the civilization's fascination with these beautiful objects led to Persia's becoming the first manufacturer of perfume. The towns and villages of the province of Fars, particularly Bishapour, Firoozabad, Kazeroon, and Shiraz, were the perfume-producing centers of Persia. Products such as perfumes; flower water from roses, sweetbrier, and eglantine; scented oils; incenses; and other perfumed materials such as musk and ambergris were exported to all corners of the world.[6]

Hollow gold fish used to hold oil or perfume

The Persian people's interest in perfume manufacturing played a part in their advances in makeup and other beauty products. They were the creators of the world's first decorative and cosmetic powders, sweet-smelling oils, and beauty creams. So groundbreaking were their makeup techniques that they inspired imitation in the Goths and Germans.[7] Kohl, used to darken the edges of the eyelids, was a favorite type of makeup.[8]

Flowers were prized for their beauty as well. They were frequently given as gifts and were also carried in bunches during festivals. Darius's personal army, The Immortals, wore crowns that were made of fragrant

The word tiara comes from the Persian word tara, which refers to the headdress worn by The Immortals. In addition to their role as the Imperial Guard, The Immortals also functioned as the standing army.

flowers and myrtle leaves. Sassanid kings prohibited their subjects from using flowers to decorate their hats, because then they would look like crowns. Monarchs were very particular about the symbolism of flowers and did not allow their companions or relatives to use the same perfumes as they did.[9]

The Significance of Hats

Some people say that one can tell a lot about a person by looking at his shoes. The same could be said of the hats people chose to wear in Persia. In addition to wearing a hat for protection and the comfort of the head, hats were worn to represent one's identity and background. One look at the hat a person was wearing and you could quickly tell his profession, race, religion, and social rank. The hat was also linked to the wearer's dignity.

Nowhere did this hold truer than with the Sassanid nobility. Over 100 crowns have been found from that period which, upon investigation, revealed the wearer's cultural, economic, and historical background. The decorations on the crowns even represented the wearer's personality traits and religious beliefs.

Ancient symbolism played an important part in the decoration used in hats. These can be broken down into the following categories: human, plant, animal, and geometrical shapes. The most popular designs were the water lily, sun, and serrated towers.

Kiana Crown

There were various types of headgear in Persia. Crowns could be closed or open and were obviously reserved for royalty. They represented the power of the monarch. Diadems were hats worn by kings on a daily basis. *Basaks* were hairband-like hats. Straight caps were worn in place of crowns. Turbanlike caps that could be wrapped around like shawls were called *dastars*. *Bashlogh* hats were hoods worn by officers, and warriors wore egg-shaped felt caps. The latter were also favored by various tribesmen. Women wore headscarves that reached their ankles. They often wore a diadem or *basak* on top of that.[10]

A turban

Cuneiform is the earliest known writing system in the world. It originated in the Sumerian civilization of southern Iraq around 3400 BCE. Cuneiform documents were formed on clay tablets by creating wedge-shaped impressions with a reed stylus. The word cuneiform, in fact, is derived from cuneus, which means "wedge" in Latin.

Traditionally children were educated at home. Trade secrets were passed down through generations by family members. Shepherds taught their children how to manage sheep, farmers taught their young how to grow crops, and cooks passed their special kitchen secrets to their children. Most peasants were illiterate, but urban merchants had basic reading and arithmetic skills.[1]

In time, a formal education system was created. Schools were of one of three types: *frahangestan* (literally 'place of education'), *dibirestan* (a school for training scribes and secretaries), and *herbedestan* (a school for religious studies). Teachers were called *hammozgar*, religious teachers were *herbed*, and instructors were *frahangbed*. Popular subjects at scribal schools were reading, writing, grammar, mathematics, and astronomy.[2] Darius made education available to all because he believed that educated subjects made for a strong empire. The curriculum was determined by the king. In return for their education, students were expected to spend some time in service to the empire.[3]

The Socratic method of instruction was common in the Sassanid Empire. Young men would sit together with their teacher and engage in discussions and debates. The location changed frequently. Students were allowed to openly disagree with the teacher. Free thinking was encouraged, and the teacher enjoyed being challenged by his students.

Education was originally imparted only to the males, while the women took care of domestic tasks. Sassanid women, however, started attending school in small numbers and accomplished a great deal in basic subjects. Some were even allowed to tackle advanced subjects like Sassanid civil law and general religious studies.[4]

In the Sassanid Empire, the syllabus was constructed around Zoroastrianism. The temple and priestly duties formed the nucleus around which academics revolved, and the value of education skyrocketed because of its association with religion. The most respected teachers were the ones who devoted all their time to learning, even pulling all-nighters while thinking about the great mysteries of life.[5]

TEACHING THE ELITE

The education that was provided to the nobility was clearly geared toward producing great thinkers, benevolent administrators, and lionhearted soldiers. It was mostly the young men who received this form of education, but their early years were spent with only women. Persian children were not allowed to interact with their fathers until after the age of five. This way if the child were to pass away young, the father would not have to endure the grief.[6]

Once the children turned five, they were ready to enter the education system. For the next fifteen years, the boys would be schooled in the areas of ethics and military tactics. Not surprisingly, Persia's strong admiration for truth-telling found its way into how the young were guided into adulthood. Along with learning horsemanship, swordsmanship, archery, and hunting, students at the royal court also learned a great deal about the execution of justice, obedience, endurance, and self-restraint. At the age of fourteen, a Persian prince was assigned to four great thinkers—the "wisest," "most just," "most temperate," and "bravest." These men tutored him in the worship of the gods, government, temperance, and courage, respectively. The young princes became

Music was an important part of Persian prayers and celebrations. One of the oldest Persian musical instruments was the tanbour, a guitar-like instrument that inspired, among others, the Indian sitar and tambura. The santour was a hammered dulcimer that is still used in Iraq, India, Egypt, and Turkey. Other popular musical instruments were drums, harps, and tambourines.

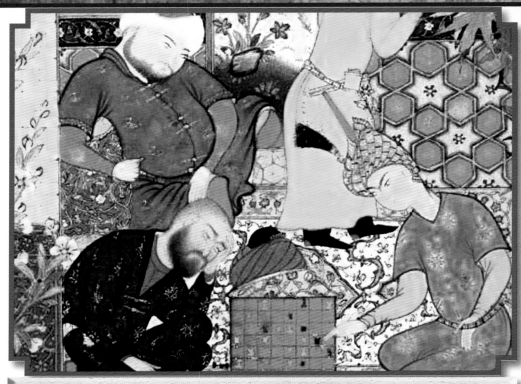

To the Persians, chess wasn't simply a game but also an art, a science, and a sport. It was seen as an abstract war game that helped strengthen the minds of the players. Some historians believe that the game itself originated in Persia. The words for checkmate, queen, and bishop all have roots in the Persian language.

highly skilled soldiers who were also exceptionally well versed in ethics.

The arts formed a large part of a prince's education. Nobles were taught the art of playing musical instruments and singing, games like chess and backgammon, and general information about wines, flowers, women, riding animals, social etiquette, ceremonial rites, conduct on festive occasions, and speech making.[7]

Darius restored a medical school at Sais in Egypt that catered to the Egyptian nobility. The college at Gundishapur that was later established by the Sassanid king Khosrau I attracted the greatest minds of that time in the fields of medicine, philosophy, and therapy. Sufi (Muslim) mysticism also found its roots at this particular school.[8]

The Persian Language

The principle language of the Persians was Farsi. The origins of the language can be traced back to 700 BCE. Farsi, or Persian, is an Indo-European language that was brought to the Iranian Plateau by the Aryans and has much in common with European languages like English, German, and French, and southern Asian languages like Sanskrit. Even though Persian is now written in the Arabic script, it is not related to Arabic or other Middle Eastern languages. Persian continues to be spoken in Iran, Afghanistan, Tajikistan, and parts of Turkey. It is also the second language of Islam.

Persian has undergone a great deal of changes since the time of the Aryans. The version called Old Persian started in the Achaemenid Empire in the sixth century BCE and lasted until the third century CE. The Sassanids communicated in Middle Persian until the tenth century CE, when New Persian was introduced.

Persia was a diverse empire, and respecting multiculturalism was the glue that held it together. Royal inscriptions and other communications were often recorded in more than one language. Elamite, Akkadian, and Aramaic were popular in the Achaemenid Empire, as were Greek, Syriac, and Parthian after that. Some of these languages are now extinct. Darius's inscriptions at the rocks at Behistun are carved primarily in Old Persian but are also accompanied by Elamite and Akkadian translations.

As Persian changed in its spoken form, so did its written representation. Old Persian was written in the cuneiform script. The Parthians and Sassanids wrote Middle Persian in the Aramaic, Parthian, Avestan, and Pahlavi scripts. The sacred texts of the Zoroastrians are written in Avestan. With

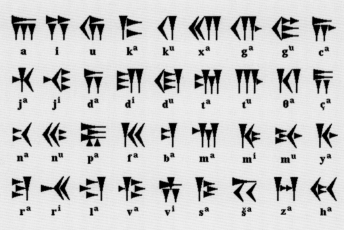

the fall of the Persian Empire, the Arabs gave new form to the language in their Arabic script.[9]

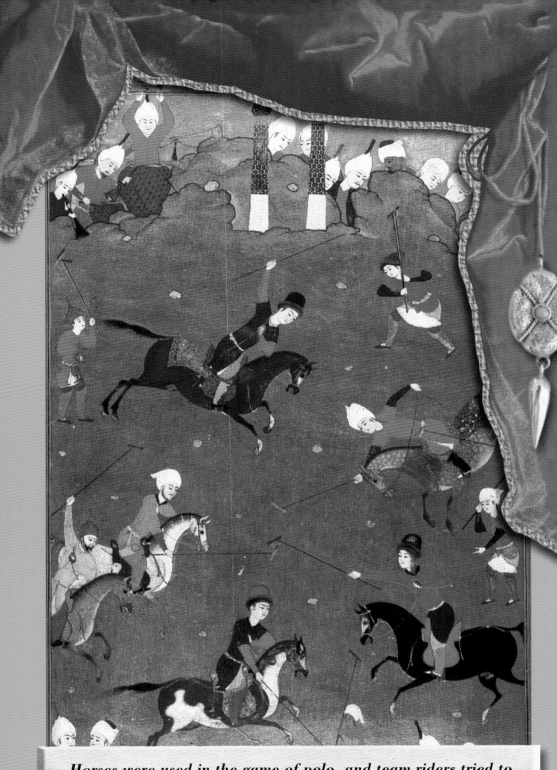

Horses were used in the game of polo, and team riders tried to hit a wooden ball across the field with a long wooden mallet, or hammer. Polo became the sport of kings and the wealthy.

HOW DID THEY HAVE FUN?

Chapter 7

Maybe the ancient Persian society had its own version of the famous saying, "All work and no play makes Jack a dull boy." While ethics, truth-telling, and going to school may sound like the basis for a serious culture, the Persians often had a lot of fun going to sporting events and festivals. They liked to work hard, but they also liked to lie back and celebrate life within their community with an equal amount of energy, which made the average year in the empire a very lively year indeed.

SPORTING EVENTS
Polo is believed to have originated in the Iranian Plateau before the reign of Darius. The sport was a favorite among the royalty and was enjoyed by kings, queens, mounted warriors, and other nobility alike. It was also played at local festivals.[1]

Another sport that is still popular is pitting animals against each other in fights. You may already know about bullfights, but the ancient Persians played this spectator sport using all kinds of creatures, including rams, buffalos, camels, guard dogs, bears, roosters, and even spiders and scorpions. Bullfights especially were very popular and were orga-nized by local governors in the central squares of their cities. They were hosted to mark the end of seasonal labor in the fields and also at marriage ceremonies. Many an important guest was honored when a bullfight was held in his name. Much ado was made of the winning bull: a ribbon would be tied around its horns, a bell fastened around its neck, and flowers scattered all over.[2]

Board games were popular as early as the Achaemenid dynasty, and they were taught as part of a noble education. Some favorites were chess, backgammon, and board games that were played with dice.[3]

The Persians took sports seriously. In addition to building physical agility and fostering good health, they trained in survival, like boot camp. Horsemanship, polo, dart throwing, wrestling, boxing, archery, and fencing were taught to youths under twenty-four under conditions of severe hardship. The trainees were being prepared for the harsh conditions of war, such as hunger, thirst, fatigue, heat, and cold.[4]

A PERSIAN NEW YEAR

The festival of Nowruz (New Day) has been ushering in the New Year for Zoroastrians for at least 2,500 years, well before the Persian Empire. It is believed that Zoroaster himself founded the festival.[5] Despite having lost most of its religious significance, Nowruz is still celebrated by the people of Iran and others of Persian heritage.

The ancient Persians celebrated Nowruz to mark the spring equinox. The people of that time lived together with nature, and the rebirth of the earth during the spring was a time of great celebration. For the Achaemenids, it seemed appropriate to observe this festival at their springtime residence, the great city of Persepolis.[6]

The royal celebration at Persepolis was quite spectacular. The king sat on his jeweled throne at his palace, receiving his subjects and gov-ernors as the various satrapies paid tribute to him. Ambassadors from nations under his control also paid their respects. The city would hum with the sounds of feasts, prayers, dance, theater performances, and jokes.

The common people spent the mornings reflecting in prayer. The rest of the day was spent visiting family and friends and entertaining guests amid great feasts and merriment.[7]

Nowruz was celebrated for five days by the ancient Persians. The sixth day, Great Nowruz (*Nowruz-e bozorg*), was celebrated as Zoroaster's birthday. The Sassanids began celebrating Nowruz 10 days before the actual festival and spent 21 days celebrating it after! Homes were cleaned to welcome Forouhars and the spirits of the dead. During the Suri Festival, bonfires were lit, and people leaped over them to bring good health for the coming year.[8]

A wall painting in Esfahan, Iran, that dates from the Safavid era depicts a Chaharshanbe Suri celebration. Now observed on the last Tuesday night of the year, the festival used to be celebrated on a Wednesday ("Chahar Shanbeh") until the Iranian revolution in 1979. Suri means "red" and refers to the bonfires that are lit to keep the sun shining all night until dawn.

CELEBRATING CREATION

The biggest festival after Nowruz was Mihregan. As Nowruz marked the renewal of spring, Mihregan marked the harvest, the end of the growing season. Celebrations were grand, especially in the royal cities. An Achaemenid king was once recorded as receiving 20,000 horses from a satrap during Mihregan festivities![9]

Zoroastrian festivals fall into two categories: the Nowruz and the six *gahambars*. The latter were originally agricultural festivals that found their way into Zoroastrianism over time. The Persians recognized six seasons, and the *gahambar* feasts were observed during the first five days of each. These were the Maidh-yo-zarem (when fresh vegetables were abundant), Maidh-yo-shema (midsummer harvest), Paiti-shahem (the fruit harvest), Aya-threm (in time to sow the winter crops), Maidh-ya-rem (the period of perfect rest), and Hamas-path-maedem (equality of heat and cold in preparation for the Nowruz).[10]

Other festivals included the Shab-e Chaleh (winter solstice, December 21), forty days before Jashn-e Sadeh. Daygan celebrated the end of the longest night of the year.[11] In addition to these, countless local festivals were celebrated all across the empire. Annual pilgrimages to shrines were also occasion for festivities. Local communities and individual families also often expressed thanksgiving in the form of spontaneous feasts.[12]

The Persian word for celebration is *jashn*, and all festivals were celebrated with equal fervor.[13] Lighting bonfires was symbolic for welcoming life and driving away the forces of evil. Priests would lead prayers as the people danced around the fire. Lavish banquets were hosted, at which storytelling, miming, music, and singing were performed. Wine flowed from every cup, and food was blessed. Chariot-racing, horseracing, and athletic contests were also held.[14]

Festivals were a time to remember the order of life, so charitable behavior was encouraged. Physical cleanliness and banishing negative thoughts were a religious duty of every Zoroastrian and were part of observing festivals. People wore their best clothes at such times, and all but necessary work was forbidden.[15]

The Calendar System

The Persians were one of the earliest civilizations to follow a solar calendar, possibly because of the symbolic importance of the sun in Zoroastrianism. Much like our modern calendar, the Persians divided the year into 12 months, and they even recognized leap years. Each month had 30 days, but there was no concept of weeks. The spring equinox marked the New Year. The origins of this calendar are unknown, but evidence points to similar calendars being used by agricultural communities on the Iranian Plateau before the time of the empire.

Months and days were named after deities and all that was good.[16] In New Persian, the months are *Farvadin, Ordibehest, Khordad, Tir, Amordad, Shahrivar, Mehr, Aban, Azar, Day, Bahman,* and *Esfand.* The first day of the month is named after Ahura Mazda. The rest are named after the Amesha Spentas, the elements (Fire, Water, Sun, Moon, Star, and Life), and the good qualities of Friendship, Obedience, Justice, Progress, Victory, Joy, Conscious, Happiness, Truth, Sky, Earth, Good Words, and Everlasting Light. The days are as follows: *Urmazd, Bahman, Ordibehesht, Sharivar, Spandarmaz, Khordad, Amordad, Day-be-Azar, Azar, Aban, Khur/Khir, Mah, Tir, Gush/Gaush, Day-be-Mehr, Mehr, Sorush, Rashn, Farvardin, Vrahram, Ram, Bad, Day-be-Din, Din, Ard (Ashi), Eshtad, Asman, Zamyad, Mantraspand,* and *Anaram.*[17] Every month had a day with the same name, and those days would be dedicated to that particular deity in the form of a festival.[18]

The Persians also measured the passage of time in eras or reigns of kings. The stars and constellations were another way the ancients kept track of time. Sundials were a popular tool for determining the time of day.

Persian astrolabe

The Iran Carpet Company holds the distinction of having created the largest handwoven carpet in the world. Muslims pray five times a day on the carpet that covers the entire floor of the main praying hall of the Sultan Qaboos Grand Mosque in Muscat, Oman. The mosque was inaugurated in May 2001.

HOW DID THEY MAKE ART?

Chapter 8

Persian carpets are one of the signature exports of the region and have been for over 2,000 years. The oldest carpet was found in Siberia and is thought to have been made by Persian nomads.[1] These handmade rugs are prized for their delicate knots, durable colors, and intricate patterns, which can never be duplicated. Rugs for everyday use are made of wool and cotton. Expensive ones are made of silk.

Techniques and patterns were passed down through generations of carpet makers by memory. These skills were especially important for women. Brides were sometimes chosen for their carpet-making talents.

Carpet designs were often geometric. Floral patterns in rectangular plots represented the ideal Persian garden, and animal and human images were also included. Colors and dyes were derived from plants and insects. The most expensive carpet in history was owned by Sassanid ruler Khosrau II and was called *Bahar-e-Kasra* ("Spring of Khosrau"). Amazingly true to life, the carpet was designed like a garden, complete with flowers, trees, and stones. Streams were made of gold and silver threads, and precious gems were woven in to represent the colors of springtime.[2]

Carpets were also used as wall decorations and to sleep on. Nomads often use them as tent doors, and Muslims use smaller carpets as prayer mats. Today the world's largest Persian carpet, the Carpet of Wonder, covers the floor of the prayer hall at the Sultan Qaboos Grand Mosque in Muscat, Oman. Weavers took four years to make the 1.7 billion knots on the 5,194-square-yard carpet![3]

ANCIENT POTTERY

Some of the oldest pottery on the Iranian Plateau has been dated to 6000 BCE. Bright colors were a main feature of Persia's oldest art. By about 1000 CE, Persian style had evolved into its distinctive geometric, floral, and animal designs. The lotus flower was a popular design representing life and women. Many jugs and jars were shaped in the form of deer, goats, or other animals.[4]

Gilded silver Sassanid vase

Many everyday objects—such as serving dishes, trays, candlesticks, and incense burners—were made of metal. Gold-plated silver cups and dishes were often decorated with scenes from life, such as a scene from a royal hunt. Coppersmiths, tinsmiths, and engravers are still common in the bazaars on the Iranian Plateau.[5]

Silver, gold, bronze, clay, and even glass were popular materials for fashioning drinking vessels. Bowls were inscribed with the name of the king and decorated with flowers. Metal bowls were sometimes made to a specific weight standard and used as currency.[6]

ROCK SCULPTURES

Persian art was derived from Egyptian, Babylonian, Assyrian, and Grecian sources but customized to the tastes of the reigning monarch. Over time, a distinct creative style emerged that the Persians

could claim as their own. The most impressive forms of art were the reliefs carved out of solid rock.

The Behistun inscriptions were commissioned by Darius in 515 BCE. These huge carvings, which are high on a cliff in the Zagros Mountains, show Ahura Mazda overseeing Darius defeating his enemies. Part of the inscriptions reads:

> "Within these lands, whosoever was a friend, him have I surely protected; whosoever was hostile, him have I utterly destroyed. By the grace of Ahura Mazda these lands have conformed to my decrees; as it was commanded unto them by me, so was it done. Ahura Mazda has granted unto me this empire. Ahura Mazda brought me help, until I gained this empire; by the grace of Ahura Mazda do I hold this empire."[7]

Reliefs can also be found at tombs. Naqsh-e-Rustam is the site of the tombs and reliefs of several Persian kings, including Darius and his Achaemenid successors, and also their Sassanid counterparts.[8] Taq-e-Bostan is one of the 30 relief sites from the Sassanid era. It depicts scenes from the coronation ceremony of Ardashir I and Shapur III, among others.[9] The reliefs at Naqsh-e-Rajab are also from the Sassanid years.[10]

Columns were frequently adorned with sculpted images of winged creatures. The palaces at Persepolis carry reliefs of the king, royal guards, and tribute bearers. The main gateway to the city is flanked by a pair of huge bulls with human heads. Susa portrays soldiers, winged bulls, sphinxes, and griffins.[11]

Persian Man-Bull Column

The Book of Kings

The *Shahnameh* is to the Persians what the *Iliad* and *Odyssey* are to the Greeks. This collection of ancient myths and legends is in poem form and was created by Hakim Abdul Qasim Ferdowsi. Ferdowsi spent thirty-five years composing the 60,000 couplets that have regaled generations of Persians with inspiring stories of the ancient kings. This book also serves as an important source of history. It starts with the creation of the world and ends with the Arab conquest of Persia.[12]

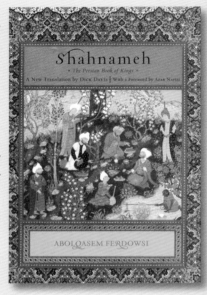

Much of the information about the earlier Persians had been lost by the time the Sassanids came to power in 226 BCE. Over the next few hundred years, many attempts were made to create the Book of Kings. The stories were collected over a period of time, but no one is really sure when the gathering started. Some stories are taken from the holy books of the Zoroastrians. Although Ferdowsi was born in the tenth century CE, his version of the *Shahnameh* is the most popular. Written in Farsi, the book is seven times as long as the *Iliad* and retains a lot of the Persian language, with its use of grand metaphors in its heroic narrative.[13]

Even today, the *Shahnameh* is considered a national treasure, a part of every Persian's ancient legacy. Schoolchildren commit parts of it to memory. The heroes of the book have even made their way to other cultures that were influenced by the Persians. The stories all revolve around the magnificence of a charismatic monarchy. Other themes in the book are loyalty to vassals, the inevitability of fate, and the battle between Good and Evil.[14]

Hakim Abdul Qasim Ferdowsi

HOW TO MAKE A HENNA TATTOO

Henna tattoos have become quite popular in the modern United States. Celebrities the world over are turning to henna (also called Mehndi) to create beautiful designs on their bodies. But henna tattoos aren't tattoos at all. Their reddish-brown color is obtained from the crushed leaves of a plant, and chemicals can be added to the mixture to obtain other colors. Henna paste produces a dye that stains the skin, and it is temporary, lasting anywhere from a week to a couple of months. Henna is mostly used to color the skin, but because of its conditioning properties, it is also used as hair dye. Henna has traditionally been used to decorate the hands and feet of women during weddings and other ceremonies, but there is no limit to how creative both boys and girls can get in making beautiful, temporary designs on their arms, legs, and wherever else people like to get tattoos!

YOU WILL NEED
Old clothes
Old newspapers
Henna powder
Water
Lemon juice
Cotton balls
Paintbrushes

INSTRUCTIONS
1. Wear old clothes to do this project, as the henna may stain them. You might also want to lay old newspapers on the table where you are working.
2. Mix the henna powder with enough water to make a yogurt-like paste.
3. Dip the paintbrush in the henna paste and use it to carefully create a design on your skin.
4. Using cotton balls, gently apply lemon juice on the henna paste as it dries on your skin. This will help bring out the color of the tattoo. Make sure you don't smudge your design or smear it on your clothes!
5. When your design has completely dried, dust the dried henna paste from your skin. Do not use water or soap for 24 hours.

BCE

c. 2000   Aryans begin to migrate from Asia to the Iranian Plateau. They eventually form the kingdoms of Medea and Fars (Persia).

c. 1000–
600   Zarathushtra (Zoroaster) is born; he founds the religion Zoroastrianism.

722   Dayaukku founds the Medean dynasty.

700   Achaemenes founds the Achaemenid dynasty.

550   The first Persian Empire begins when Achaemenid king Cyrus the Great brings Medea under Persian control.

522 BC–
486 BC   Darius I is king; he founds Persepolis, the new capital of Persia; sets up a universal legal system called the *Data*; divides the kingdom into provinces called satrapies; and constructs the Royal Road.

500   Aramaic becomes the official language of the Persian Empire.

499–450   Persia and Greece fight the Persian Wars; Ionia and Thrace, which are parts of Greece, gain independence from Persia.

330   The Achaemenid dynasty ends when Alexander the Great conquers Persia and destroys Persepolis.

329   Artaxerxes V dies. He is the last of the Achaemenids.

305   Seleucus Nicator takes control of Persia, and the Seleucid Empire begins. Its capital is in Seleucia (Iraq).

250   The Seleucid Empire is overthrown by the second Persian Empire (also called the Parthian Empire), founded by the Aryan tribe of Parni. Its capital is Ctesiphon, near Seleucia. Zervanism becomes a popular religion.

CE

226   A tribe from Fars founds the third and last Persian Empire, called the Sassanid Empire. Ardashir becomes the first Sassanid king. The power of the Magi reaches its height during this empire.

226–241   The Avesta is compiled.

244   Sassanid king Shapur I attacks Rome.

276   Mani is executed. He had introduced Manichaeism, which tried to incorporate Judaism, Christianity, and Zoroastrianism into one religion.

528   The religion Mazdakism fails to catch on. It tried to abolish private property, to divide wealth, and to promote nonviolence and vegetarianism.

531   Khosrau I becomes the Sassanid king. He will build the Palace of the Great Arch in Ctesiphon in 560.

614   The Sassanids capture Jerusalem.

619   The Sassanids capture Egypt.

627   Sassanid king Khosrau II is defeated by Roman emperor Heraclitus.

628   Khosrau II is assassinated by his troops. The Romans retake Syria.

636   The Arabs capture Ctesiphon, and the Sassanid Empire ends.

651   The Persian Empire falls when Arabs, under the caliphate of Uthman ibn 'Affan, complete their invasion from the south. Islam becomes the dominant religion.

697   The Arabs force the Persians to use Arabic script instead of the Pahlavi alphabet.

850   Persian mathematician Al-Khwarizmi, the father of algebra and inventor of Arabic numerals, dies.

c. 1000   Hakim Abdul Qasim Ferdowsi records the *Shahnameh* (Book of Kings).

1274   Persian astronomer Nasir Al-Din Tusi builds the Maraghah observatory.

1935   General Reza Khan changes Persia's name to Iran.

CHAPTER NOTES

Chapter 1 How Did They Build the Empire?
1. Helen Loveday, Bruce Wannell, Christopher Baumer, and Bijan Omrani, *Iran–Persia: Ancient and Modern* (Sheung Wan, Hong Kong: Odyssey Books and Guides, 2005), pp. 22–48.
2. Ibid.
3. Sandra Mackey, *The Iranians: Persia, Islam, and The Soul of a Nation* (New York: Dutton, 1996), pp. 22–23.
4. Elton L. Daniel, *The History of Iran* (Westport, Conn.: Greenwood Press, 2001), pp. 15, 42.
5. Rüdiger Sshmitt, "The Achaemenids Law, *Data*," http://www.cais-soas.com/CAIS/Law/data.htm
6. Loveday, et al.
7. Ibid.
8. Mackey.
9. Ibid.
10. Loveday, et al.
11. William H. Forbis, *Fall of the Peacock Throne: The Story of Iran* (New York: Harper & Row, 1980), pp. 10–30.
12. Daniel.
13. Muhammad A. Dandamayev, "Economy in the Achaemenid Iran," http://www.cais-soas.com/CAIS/Law/economy_achaemenid.htm
14. Rika Gyselen, "Economy in the Sasanian Iran," http://www.cais-soas.com/CAIS/Law/economy_sasanian.htm
15. Dandamayev.
16. Gianpaolo Savoia-Vizzini, "An Introduction to the Empire of Sasanian Dynasty," http://www.cais-soas.com/CAIS/History/Sasanian/sasanid.htm
17. Mohammad Sadegh Nazmi Afshar, "Insurance in Ancient Iran," http://www.cais-soas.com/CAIS/History/insurance.htm
18. John Curtis, *Ancient Persia* (Cambridge, Mass.: Harvard University Press, 1990), pp. 37–38.
19. Darius Jahanian, "The First Declaration of Human Rights," http://www.cais-soas.com/CAIS/Culture/human_rights.htm
20. Ancient Persia, *Cyrus's Cylinder*, http://www.ancientpersia.com/ppl/cylinder.htm
21. Jahanian.
22. Mackey.
23. PersianEmpire.info: *The Achaemenid Empire*, Death of Cyrus, http://persianempire.info/cyrusdeath.htm

Chapter 2 How Did They Practice Religion?
1. Helen Loveday, Bruce Wannell, Christopher Baumer, and Bijan Omrani, *Iran–Persia: Ancient and Modern* (Sheung Wan, Hong Kong: Odyssey Books and Guides, 2005), pp. 164-168.
2. Ancient Persia, *Ancient Persia Religion*, http://www.ancientpersia.com/religion/rlg_f.htm
3. Loveday, et al.
4. William G. Doty, *World Mythology* (New York: Barnes and Noble Books, 2002), pp. 34–35.
5. John R. Hinnells, *Persian Mythology* (New York: Peter Bedrick Books, 1985), pp. 6–21.
6. Loveday, et al.
7. Doty.
8. Loveday, et al.
9. Ibid.
10. Hinnells.
11. Loveday, et al.
12. Ibid.

13. Ibid.
14. Hinnells.

Chapter 3 How Did They Build Their Cities?
1. Helen Loveday, Bruce Wannell, Christopher Baumer, and Bijan Omrani, *Iran–Persia: Ancient and Modern* (Sheung Wan, Hong Kong: Odyssey Books and Guides, 2005), p. 130.
2. Ibid.
3. History.com, *Iranian Art and Architecture*, http://www.history.com/encyclopedia.do?articleId=212862
4. Ibid.
5. Achaemenid Persia, *Houses*, http://members.ozemail.com.au/~ancientpersia/houses.html
6. Iransaga, *The Persian Garden*, http://www.artarena.force9.co.uk/pgarden.htm
7. Mehrdad Fakour, "Achaemenid gardens," http://www.cais-soas.com/CAIS/Culture/achaemenid_gardens.htm
8. Ibid.
9. Ibid.
10. Elton L. Daniel, *The History of Iran* (Westport, Conn.: Greenwood Press, 2001), p. 42.
11. Ibid.
12. William H. Forbis, *Fall of the Peacock Throne: The Story of Iran* (New York: Harper & Row, 1980), pp. 10–30.
13. Daniel.

Chapter 4 How Did They Run Their Society?
1. Djalal Khaleqi-Motlaq, "Iranian Etiquette in the Sassanian Period," http://www.cais-soas.com/CAIS/Culture/etiquette_sasanian.htm
2. Ibid.
3. Ibid.
4. Pallan R. Ichaporia, "Customs, Rules & Correct Manners in Shah-Nameh," http://www.cais-soas.com/CAIS/Literature/Shahnameh/customs_rules_Shahnameh.htm
5. Gianpaolo Savoia-Vizzini, "An Introduction to the Empire of Sasanian Dynasty," http://www.cais-soas.com/CAIS/History/Sasanian/sasanid.htm
6. Ibid.
7. Ibid.
8. Ibid.
9. Massoume Price, "Women's Lives in Ancient Persia," http://www.iranonline.com/History/Women%27s-Lives/index.html
10. The British Museum: Forgotten Empire—The world of Ancient Persia, *Dining*. http://www.thebritishmuseum.ac.uk/forgottenempire/luxury/dining.html
11. Touraj Daryaee, "The Art of Wine in Ancient Persia," http://www.cais-soas.com/CAIS/Culture/wine_good.htm
12. Rika Gyselen, "Economy in Sasanian Iran," http://www.cais-soas.com/CAIS/Law/economy_sasanian.htm
13. Robert C. Henrickson, "Economy in Pre-Achaemenid Iran," http://www.cais-soas.com/CAIS/Law/economy_pre_achaemenid.htm
14. Stanley Insler, "The Love of Truth in Pre-Islamic Iran," http://www.cais-soas.com/CAIS/Culture/love_of_truth.htm
15. Ibid.

Chapter 5 How Did They Dress?

1. Gianpaolo Savoia-Vizzini, "An Introduction to the Empire of Sasanian Dynasty," http://www.cais-soas. com/CAIS/History/Sasanian/sasanid.htm
2. Ibid.
3. Mohammad Sadegh Nazmi Afshar, "Insurance in Ancient Iran," http://www.cais-soas.com/CAIS/ History/insurance.htm
4. Djalal Khaleqi-Motlaq, "Iranian Etiquette in the Sassanian Period," http://www.cais-soas.com/CAIS/ Culture/etiquette_sasanian.htm
5. The British Museum: Forgotten Empire—The world of Ancient Persia, Jewellery, http://www. thebritishmuseum.ac.uk/forgottenempire/luxury/ jewellery.html
6. M. Hossein Abrishami, "Historical Background of Perfume & Perfume Manufacturing in Iran," http://www.cais-soas.com/CAIS/Women/perfume. htm
7. Ibid.
8. British Museum.
9. Abrishami.
10. Masood Partovi, "A Research on Ancient Iranian Dress," http://www.cais-soas.com/CAIS/Costume_ and_Textile/hat.htm

Chapter 6 How Did They School Themselves?

1. Franklin T. Burroughs, "Cultural Factors in the Education of Ancient Iran," http://www.cais-soas. com/CAIS/Culture/cultural_factors_education.htm
2. Ahmad Tafazzoli, "Education Under the Parthian & Sasanian Dynasties," http://www.cais-soas.com/ CAIS/Culture/education_partho_sasanid.htm
3. Burroughs.
4. Ibid.
5. Ibid.
6. Muhammad A. Dandamayev, "Achaemenid Education System," http://www.cais-soas.com/ CAIS/Culture/education_achaemenid.htm
7. Tafazzoli.
8. Ibid.
9. Shapour Suren-Pahlav, "Iranian Languages & Literature," http://www.cais-soas.com/CAIS/ Languages/iranian_languages.htm

Chapter 7 How Did They Have Fun?

1. Shapour Suren-Pahlav, "History of Choghan (Polo)," http://www.cais-soas.com/CAIS/Sport/polo. htm
2. Christian Bromberger, "Gâvbâzî (Bull Fighting)," http://www.cais-soas.com/CAIS/Sport/gavbazi.htm
3. Shapour Suren-Pahlav, "Chess; Iranian or Indian Invention?" http://www.cais-soas.com/CAIS/Sport/ chess.htm
4. Nurbakhsh Rahimzadeh, "Zarathushtra; The First Monotheist Prophet," http://www.cais-soas.com/ CAIS/Religions/iranian/Zarathushtrian/first_ prophet.htm
5. Ali A. Jafari, "Noruz (New Day); The New Year of the Iranian Peoples," http://www.cais-soas.com/ CAIS/Celebrations/noruz.htm
6. Ibid.
7. Keikhosrow Mobed, "Iranian Zoroastrian (Zartoshti) Festivals and Rituals," http://zoreled.org/Iranzorfestrit.aspx

8. Massoume Price, "Iranian New Year No Ruz," http://www.iranonline.com/festivals/Iranian-new-year/index.html
9. Massoume Price, "Mihregan (Mehregan)," http://www.iranonline.com/festivals/mehregan-english-2/index.html
10. Fariborz Rahnamoon, "Calendar in Ancient Iran," http://ahura.homestead.com/files/IranZaminEleven/ Fariborz_Calendar_in_Ancient_Iran_E11.pdf
11. Massoume Price, "Shab e Cheleh (Yalda Festival)," http://www.iranonline.com/festivals/yalda-english/ index.html
12. Mary Boyce, "Zarathushtrian Festivals," http:// www.cais-soas.com/CAIS/Religions/iranian/ Zarathushtrian/zarathushtras_festivals.htm
13. Rahnamoon.
14. Boyce.
15. Ibid.
16. Massoume Price, "Iranian Months, Origin of The Names," http://www.iranonline.com/festivals/ Persian-months/index.html
17. CAIS, Zoroastrian Calendar, http://www.cais-soas. com/CAIS/Religions/iranian/Zarathushtrian/ zoroastrian_calendar.htm
18. Rahnamoon.

Chapter 8 How Did They Make Art?

1. Helen Loveday, Bruce Wannell, Christopher Baumer, and Bijan Omrani, Iran—Persia: Ancient and Modern (Sheung Wan, Hong Kong: Odyssey Books and Guides, 2005), pp. 46, 156–158.
2. M. G. Morony, "Bahar-e Kasra," http://www.cais-soas.com/CAIS/Art/Decorative-Arts/Persian-Carpet/baharestan_carpet.htm
3. Oriental Rugs the O'Connell Guide, The Carpet of Wonder—The Processes of Weaving, http://www. persiancarpetguide.com/sw-asia/Rugs/Rug988.htm
4. Stanley Kohen, "The Mountain Goat; Symbol of Rain in Iranian Pottery," http://www.cais-soas.com/ CAIS/Mythology/mount_goat.htm
5. Sandra Mackey, The Iranians: Persia, Islam, and The Soul of a Nation (New York: Dutton, 1996), pp. 62–65.
6. The British Museum: Forgotten Empire— The world of Ancient Persia, Dining, http://www.thebritishmuseum.ac.uk/ forgottenempire/luxury/dining.html
7. The Circle of Ancient Iranian Studies, Inscription of Darius the Great at Behistun, http://www.cais-soas. com/CAIS/Languages/aryan/inscription_of_darius_ grt.htm
8. Jona Lendering, "Naqs-I Rustam," http://www. livius.org/na-nd/naqsh-i-rustam/naqsh-i-rustam.html
9. Jona Lendering, "Taq-e Bostan," http://www.livius. org/a/iran/taqebostan/taqebostan1.html
10. Jona Lendering, "Naqs-e Rajab," http://www.livius. org/a/iran/naqs-e_rajab/reliefs.html
11. History.com, Iranian Art and Architecture, http://www.history.com/encyclopedia. do?articleId=212862
12. Mackey.
13. Ibid.
14. Loveday, et al.

FURTHER READING

Books
Cartlidge, Cherese. *Iran*. San Diego, California: Lucent Books, 2002.
Habeeb, William Mark. *Iran*. Broomall, Pennsylvania: Mason Crest Publishers, 2004.
Milivojevic, JoAnn. *Iran: Enchantment of the World*. New York: Children's Press, 2008.
Rajendra, Vijeya, Gisela Kaplan, and Rudi Rajendra. *Iran*. Tarrytown, New York: Benchmark
    Books, 2004.
Taus-Bolstad, Stacy. *Iran in Pictures*. Minneapolis, Minnesota: Lerner Publications Company, 2004.

Works Consulted
This book is based on the author's e-mail correspondence with Farshid Mojaver Hosseini,
professor of economics at University of California–Davis, and on the following sources:

Ancient Persia http://www.ancientpersia.com/
The British Museum: Forgotten Empire–The World of Ancient Persia
    http://www.thebritishmuseum.ac.uk/forgottenempire/
Circle of Ancient Iranian Studies http://www.cais-soas.com/CAIS/frontpage.htm
Curtis, John. *Ancient Pearsia*. Cambridge, Massachusetts: Harvard University Press, 1990.
Daniel, Elton L. *The History of Iran*. Westport, Connecticut: Greenwood Press, 2001.
Doty, William G. *World Mythology*. New York: Barnes and Noble Books, 2002.
Forbis, William H. *Fall of the Peacock Throne: The Story of Iran*. New York: Harper & Row: 1980.
Hinnells, John R. *Persian Mythology*. New York: Peter Bedrick Books, 1985.
Internet Ancient History Sourcebook http://www.fordham.edu/halsall/ancient/asbook.html
Lendering, Jona. "Naqs-e Rajab," http://www.livius.org/a/iran/naqs-e_rajab/reliefs.html
———. "Naqs-I Rustam," http://www.livius.org/na-nd/naqsh-i-rustam/naqsh-i-rustam.html
———. "Taq-e Bostan," http://www.livius.org/a/iran/taqebostan/taqebostan1.html
Loveday, Helen, Bruce Wannell, Christopher Baumer, and Bijan Omrani. *Iran–Persia: Ancient and
    Modern*. Sheung Wan, Hong Kong: Odyssey Books and Guides, 2005.
Mackey, Sandra. *The Iranians: Persia, Islam, and the Soul of a Nation*. New York: Dutton, 1996.
Mobed, Keikhosrow. "Iranian Zoroastrian (Zartoshti) Festivals and Rituals," http://zoreled.org/
    Iranzorfestrit.aspx
PersianEmpire.info: *The Achaemenid Empire*, Death of Cyrus, http://persianempire.info/cyrusdeath.
    htm
Price, Massoume. "Shab e Cheleh (Yalda Festival)," http://www.iranonline.com/festivals/yalda-
    english/index.html
———. "Women's Lives in Ancient Persia," http://www.iranonline.com/History/Women%27s-
    Lives/index.html
Rahnamoon, Fariborz. "Calendar in Ancient Iran," http://ahura.homestead.com/files/
    IranZaminEleven/Fariborz_Calendar_in_Ancient_Iran_E11.pdf

On the Internet
Achaemenid Persia
    http://members.ozemail.com.au/~ancientpersia/index.html
BBC: Religion & Ethics–Zoroastrianism
    http://www.bbc.co.uk/religion/religions/zoroastrian/
Farvardyn
    http://www.farvardyn.com/
Iransaga
    http://www.artarena.force9.co.uk/iran.htm
Magic of Persia
    http://www.magicofpersia.com/

cataphract (KAA-tuh-frakt)—A heavily armed and armored cavalryman.

cavalry (KAH-vul-ree)—An army troop mounted on horseback.

citadel (SIH-tuh-del)—A fortress that commands a city.

clibanarii (klih-buh-NAHR-ee)—A military unit of heavily armored horsemen.

conduits (KON-doo-its)—Natural or artificial channels through which something (such as water) is conveyed.

cuneiform (kyoo-NEE-ih-form)—Composed of or written in wedge-shaped characters.

diaspora (dy-AS-por-uh)—People who settled far from their ancestral homelands.

dynasty (DY-nuh-stee)—A succession of rulers of the same line of descent.

etiquette (EH-tih-ket)—The conduct or procedure required by good breeding or prescribed by authority to be observed in social or official life.

faience (FAY-unts)—Earthenware decorated with opaque colored glazes.

Forouhars (foh-ROO-hars)—Guardian angels.

griffins—Mythical animals typically having the head, forepart, and wings of an eagle and the body, hind legs, and tail of a lion.

guru (GOO-roo)—A person with knowledge or expertise, especially one who is an expert in religious matters.

haute couture (oht koh-TOOR)—High fashion.

incense (IN-sents)—Material used to produce a fragrant odor when burned.

irrigation (eer-ih-GAY-shun)—The watering of farmland for growing crops.

infantry (IN-fun-tree)—Soldiers trained, armed, and equipped to fight on foot.

monotheistic (mah-noh-thee-IS-tik)—Believing that there is just one god.

mysticism (MIH-stih-sih-zum)—The belief that direct knowledge of God, spiritual truth, or ultimate reality can be attained through subjective experience (as intuition or insight).

nomads (NOH-mads)—People who have no fixed home but move from place to place, usually seasonally and within a certain area.

relief (ree-LEEF)—A sculpture in which forms and figures are carved from a flat rock.

rhyton (plural: rhyta)—Any of various fancy drinking vessels of ancient times typically shaped in part like an animal or animal's head.

satrap (SAY-trap)—The governor of a province (satrapy [SAY-truh-pee]) of ancient Persia.

sphinx (SFINKS)—One of the winged female monsters in Greek mythology that had a woman's head and a lion's body.

tribute—Payment by one ruler or nation to another to show submission and as the price of protection.

vassals—People under the protection of a feudal lord, to whom they have vowed to be faithful.

ABOUT THE AUTHOR

Khadija Ejaz was born in Lucknow, India, and was raised in Muscat, Sultanate of Oman. She earned her bachelor's and master's degrees in Computer Science and Management Information Systems at the Oklahoma State University, Stillwater, and now lives between India, Oman, and Canada. A full-time IT professional, she freelances as a writer and has numerous writing credits to her name. Her other interests include filmmaking, acting, photography, volunteer work, and the theater. To learn more about Khadija, visit her website at http://khadijaejaz.netfirms.com.